The Thomas Jefferson Center Foundation

Spending
and
Deficits

James C. Miller III

The G. Warren Nutter Lectures in Political Economy

The G. Warren Nutter Lectures in Political Economy

The G. Warren Nutter Lectures in Political Economy were instituted to honor the memory of the late Professor Nutter, to encourage scholarly interest in the range of topics to which he devoted his career, and to provide his students and associates an additional contact with each other and with the rising generation of scholars.

At the time of his death in January 1979, G. Warren Nutter was director of the Thomas Jefferson Center Foundation, adjunct scholar of the American Enterprise Institute, director of AEI's James Madison Center, a member of advisory groups at both the Hoover Institution and The Citadel, and Paul Goodloe McIntire Professor of Economics at the University of Virginia.

Professor Nutter made notable contributions to price theory, the assessment of monopoly and competition, the study of the Soviet economy, and the economics of defense and foreign policy. He earned his Ph.D. degree at the University of Chicago. In 1957 he joined with James M. Buchanan to establish the Thomas Jefferson Center for Studies in Political Economy at the University of Virginia. In 1967 he established the Thomas Jefferson Center Foundation as a separate entity but with similar objectives of supporting scholarly work and graduate study in political economy and holding conferences of economists from the United States and both Western and Eastern Europe. He served during the 1960s as director of the Thomas Jefferson Center and chairman of the Department of Economics at the University of Virginia and, from 1969 to 1973, as assistant secretary of defense for international security affairs.

James C. Miller III delivered the fourteenth G. Warren Nutter Lecture at the American Enterprise Institute for Public Policy Research, Washington, D.C., on October 15, 1986. Earlier lectures were delivered by John H. Moore, Richard A. Ware, William F. Ford, Lawrence S. Eagleburger, Roger E. Shields, Paul Craig Roberts, Yuan-li Wu, James M. Buchanan, Thomas H. Moorer, George J. Stigler, R. H. Coase, Milton Friedman, and S. Herbert Frankel.

The American Enterprise Institute
1150 17th Street, N.W.
Washington, D.C. 20036

Spending and Deficits

James C. Miller III

James C. Miller III is the director of the Office of Management and Budget.

ISBN 0-8447-1382-1

Printed in the United States of America

American Enterprise Institute for Public Policy Research
1150 Seventeenth Street, N.W., Washington, D.C. 20036

Introduction

Robert D. Tollison
Professor of Economics
George Mason University

I have known Jim Miller for twenty years. We were in the Ph.D. program together at the University of Virginia. We marched down the Lawn, side by side, to receive our doctoral degrees on a sweltering summer day laced with a thundershower in June 1969. We, like our colleagues in the Virginia graduate program in economics at the time, were profoundly influenced by our education at the feet of teachers such as James M. Buchanan and G. Warren Nutter.

Many of the students who came out of the Virginia program during those days have done extremely well as scholars, lawyers, corporate executives, government officials, and the like. A small list would include Otto Davis, Charles Plott, Charles Goetz, John Moore, Richard Wagner, John Peterman, Jack Snow, Mark Pauly, Tom Willett, Craig Stubblebine, Jack Albertine, Roger Shields, and many others too numerous to mention. A list of their professional accomplishments would compare favorably with those of the students in any other graduate economics program in the United States at the time. Jim Miller could have chosen any of these routes to success and done well. He chose instead a different route. To use Gordon Tullock's phrase, he chose to do well by doing good.

In a way, Jim is an odd result of his education. Public choice teaches that government is neither perfect nor perfectible and that the idea that people work for the public interest as opposed to their personal private interest is far removed from the reality of day-to-day, election-to-election government. Jim is a glaring exception to such maxims. What Jim Miller took from his economics training was the idea that economics could be used to promote a more rational and effective economy and that, generally, economic freedom within rules, rather than government programs that stifle individual initiative and responsibility, was the key to sound economic policy. As his career evolved, from academia to government, to think tank and back to government, Jim Miller has focused his immense energies on applying this vision of political economy to promote a better world.

In this regard, Jim has been very skillful and very fortunate. His ability as an economic analyst is unquestioned. He has written extensively on the economics of public policy issues ranging from the military draft, to airline regulation and deregulation, to economic regulation generally, to antitrust enforcement, to budgetary policy. He has even made an insightful argument about how to improve the functioning of representative democracy through computer voting.

Jim has also been fortunate. By this I mean that he has lived and worked in government at a time when the relative value of his skills, knowledge, and abilities was high. Who else, after all, had a lifesized poster of Ronald Reagan, posed as a gunslinger from the Old West, prominently displayed on his office wall in 1967? Jim has been at the center of many important policy debates over the past several years. He was a significant analyst and participant in the successful effort to deregulate U.S. airlines. He organized and implemented Executive Order 12291, instituting Office of Management and Budget oversight of the federal rule-making process. He took over the Federal Trade Commission at a time when it was widely viewed as being out of control and, in short order, put the agency back on a saner course. He is now a major player in the "battle of the budget," where his unique background in Virginia political economy has led him to support initiatives by Congress and the president (such as Gramm-Rudman-Hollings) to precommit themselves to a plan for budget balance. Jim understands the difference between behavior with and behavior without constraints. Any one of these accomplishments would be enough for the career of the rest of us. And, remember, Jim is still a young man.

History, then, has been kind to Jim Miller, who will surely go down as one of the most significant public servants of the Reagan era. He is not a creature of the media, nor is he a creature of the Congress where the natural inclination is to make deals. Jim figures out what the best policy for the country is and works to reach that goal. He is that rare individual who has done well by doing good.

I would be remiss in closing if I did not add a personal note about the private Jim Miller. The public success of some people comes at the expense of their private success. The correlation in Jim's case goes in exactly the opposite direction. Over the years, Jim and Demaris Miller have been outstanding examples of what marriage partners and parents should be. My admiration for Jim extends equally to Demaris, and you will not meet three better young people than Katrina, Felix, and Sabrina Miller. Good things do sometimes go together, and in his personal life, Jim Miller has also done well by doing good.

Spending and Deficits

James C. Miller III

Thank you, Bob. It is indeed an honor that you agreed to introduce me. As you mentioned, those of us privileged to be at the University of Virginia in the middle and late 1960s shared a very special time. Of all the students from that heyday, I think you perhaps best represent the hopes and aspirations we all shared. Over the past twenty years some of us have produced a fairly respectable manuscript now and then. You produce reams of them every year. Some of us have been fortunate to have had a few good students. You, as well as Jim Buchanan, have a legion of them—and I count myself fortunate to be a foot solider in both!

Ladies and gentlemen, we are here today to honor the memory of G. Warren Nutter. I dare say he touched the lives of almost everyone in this room; I know he touched mine. A person of commanding intellect, unwavering character, and a self-confidence born of assurance that he knew his facts. Warren did not let go of anything until he mastered it. He knew more about concentration in U.S. industry than anyone else because he conceptualized the issues, read the literature, and did the number-crunching necessary to answer his questions—all the while meeting his standards, not someone else's. When, in the wake of Sputnik, the intellectual elite—or should I say effete?—of this country were praising the Soviet economic system and its potential for overtaking the West, it was Nutter who said, "Hold the presses; has anyone looked at the facts?" And when Nutter

I would like to express my appreciation to Tom Lenard for his advice and suggestions in the preparation of this lecture and to Bob Tollison for his comments on an earlier draft. The usual caveat applies. Portions of this address have been adapted from remarks I made before a seminar sponsored by the Federal Trade Commission. See *The Political Economy of Regulation: Private Interests in the Regulatory Process* (Washington, D.C.: Federal Trade Commission, 1984), p. 293; the National Press Club (November 1, 1985); and the U.S. Chamber of Commerce (July 17, 1986).

published his massive NBER study, a lot of people had a good deal of explaining to do.[1]

But probably no matter occupied Warren more, especially toward the end of his life, than the growth of government in the West. Like Thomas Jefferson, Warren Nutter saw the gradual encroachment of government as the greatest and most pernicious threat to individual liberty. He could understand how authoritarian regimes like Nazi Germany and Communist Russia come to power—through trickery, intimidation, and violence—but he was perplexed why stable, civilized societies, in some cases with democratic institutions stretching back hundreds of years, would succumb to increasing collective domination.

Nutter had only begun his massive work on this issue when a tragic death cut short his efforts. How fortunate might we have been if Nutter had been able to finish his work! We are now left to pick up the pieces, and no doubt most of us in this room, in our own personal writings, are in one way or another groping with the question Nutter articulated for us. And it is to this issue I will turn in my remarks.

But first, let me share with you a few personal thoughts about Warren. Beneath that calculating exterior beat a heart of gold. Let me illustrate. Not to be terribly outdone by fellow graduate students Tom Willett, Mark Pauly, and others who had already broken into the big journals, in late 1967 I spotted what I perceived to be a flaw in a piece in the *American Economic Review* and dashed off a note. Wisely, I sought Mr. Nutter's counsel. "You may be right," he said, "but you've got to rewrite it to make the argument much clearer; otherwise, you don't have a chance of getting it accepted." I did rewrite it, but Nutter was not satisfied so he rewrote it himself. And then I worked on it some more, and Nutter rewrote it again. "Mr. Nutter," I said, "this is as much your note as mine, so I insist you share authorship." But Nutter would have none of that. When the note was accepted—to everyone's amazement, including mine—and appeared in the *AER*, it carried the usual footnote reference to Nutter's assistance, as well as appreciation to Roger Sherman and Tom Willett; but that is all the acknowledgment Nutter would accept.[2]

Let me share a second anecdote. In the fall of 1966 I took Nutter's

---

1. G. Warren Nutter, *Growth of Industrial Production in the Soviet Union* (Princeton: Princeton University Press for the National Bureau of Economic Research, 1962).

2. James C. Miller III, "A Paradox on Profits and Factor Prices: Comment," *American Economic Review* (September, 1968), pp. 917–19.

211 Price Theory course and did fairly well. But the next spring I met my match in Nutter's 154, Economic Growth of the Soviet Union. The problem was not economics, but history. I have never been particularly good at memorization, but the large number of history graduate students taking the course most certainly were. Moreover, this was at a time when several of us graduate students were getting under way our book on the volunteer army, and I was somewhat distracted.[3] Anyway, when grades were handed out I got a "B." Not particularly surprised, but somewhat upset over what this might mean for my career, I sought Mr. Nutter's counsel, not really holding out much hope he would change the grade. Nutter was very understanding but explained that my exams simply did not measure up to an "A" or even a "B + ." Before I left, however, he put everything in perspective. "I know how you feel," he said. "Milton Friedman once gave me a 'B'." Somehow this made everything all right.

As I said earlier, Warren Nutter was very concerned about the growth of government and wrote one of his last books on the subject.[4] That book came to mind as I was reading my predecessor's account of his experiences as budget director, shortly after I inherited the job.[5]

Undoubtedly, many of you have read at least excerpts of David Stockman's book and have formed your own opinions of it. In my view, after one gets past the anecdotes, Stockman's message is clear: if the most conservative president in two generations, supported by perhaps the smartest and most zealous budget director ever (my characterization, not his), cannot succeed at trimming government spending, then it simply cannot be done. Politicians—no matter how much in favor of smaller government they profess to be—will reflect their constituents', if not "special," interests and vote for new programs and the continuation of old ones. This inexorably leads to ever-larger government.

Let me say first that I think David Stockman had considerably more success than one would gather from reading his book. But it is also clear that we have a problem—a problem characteristic of virtually all modern democracies.

3. James C. Miller III et al., *Why the Draft?: The Case for a Volunteer Army* (New York: Penguin Books, Inc., 1968).
4. G. Warren Nutter, *Growth of Government in the West* (Washington, D.C.: American Enterprise Institute for Public Policy Research, 1978).
5. David A. Stockman, *The Triumph of Politics: Why the Reagan Revolution Failed* (New York: Harper and Row, Publishers, 1986).

The Growth of Government

Let me illustrate the nature of that problem. In 1940, just before the start of World War II, the federal government accounted for 10 percent of gross national product (GNP). This figure grew to 16 percent by 1950, 20 percent by 1970, and reached 24 percent by 1985.[6]

This rising percentage of GNP went primarily to finance an increasingly elaborate array of domestic programs. From the early 1950s, total nondefense spending grew from about 30 percent of the budget to over 70 percent at the present time.[7]

Nutter's review of the data on spending at all levels of government shows an even more dramatic rise in the percentage of national income attributable to government because of greater increases at the state and local levels.[8]

These trends are not unique to the United States.[9] During the twenty-five year period covered by the data Nutter assembled for his book, 1950 through 1974, total government expenditures for the Organization for Economic Cooperation and Development (OECD) countries rose from about 30 percent of national income to about 50 percent—and this as a result of increases in domestic spending. "External" expenditures (mainly defense) were relatively constant, in the 5–6 percent range.

Increased Reliance on Deficit Financing

At the same time that government has been taking an increasing portion of total output, the share of this take financed by debt has also risen. For the first 150 years of our history, the prevailing, indeed unquestioned, belief was that the federal budget should be balanced.[10] While deficits were unavoidable in wartime, all political parties, all presidents, and nearly all members of Congress operated on the assumption that the "norm" would be budgetary balance and even surpluses to repay some of the debt accumulated during wars. We ran surpluses for twenty-eight consecutive years after the War

---

6. *Historical Tables, Budget of the United States Government, 1987* (Washington, D.C.: U.S. Government Printing Office, 1986), table 1.2.

7. Ibid., table 6.2.

8. Nutter, *Growth of Government*, pp. 13–18.

9. Ibid., pp. 3–13.

10. Richard E. Wagner, Robert D. Tollison, Alvin Rabushka, and John T. Noonan, Jr., *Balanced Budgets, Fiscal Responsibility, and the Constitution* (Washington, D.C.: Cato Institute, 1982).

between the States, and for eleven consecutive years after World War I, amazing as that may seem.

The first erosion of this article of faith came with the emergence of fashionable forms of Keynesian economics, which made deficits not only acceptable but even desirable during recessions.[11] In the period after World War II, however, when this idea gradually became the conventional wisdom, it was also assumed that in times of prosperity the budget would be in surplus—that is, the budget would be balanced over the so-called business cycle. And as we look back, up until the late 1960s this rule was roughly observed. Our deficits, when we had them, were quite small, and we even ran a few surpluses in the 1940s and the 1950s.

Starting with the war in Vietnam, however, and continuing long after the war wound down, even this degree of discipline began slipping away. Deficits gradually ceased to be a respectable countercyclical tool and turned into an escape valve for lack of political will or for political gridlock. We are now in a situation where the deficit is large, chronic, and structural—something that is characteristic of most modern democracies. The deficit was approximately $225 billion, or some 5.4 percent of GNP, in FY 1986, at a time of modest, though respectable, economic growth and reasonably high employment. It is not only that we have had deficits in twenty-five of the past twenty-six years; more important, recently they have become much larger—in excess of 2.5 percent of GNP in all but one of the past ten years.

Nonbudgetary Spending

It is easy to focus on budget figures because they are readily available. The government's claim on the nation's resources, however, is substantially larger than is reflected in those totals. Much of this additional spending bypasses the congressional appropriations process and, therefore, does not receive the scrutiny normally accorded spending programs.[12] Much of it, moreover, represents increased liabilities for future generations, similar to public borrowing. But this

11. See James M. Buchanan and Richard E. Wagner, *Democracy in Deficit: The Political Legacy of Lord Keynes* (New York: Academic Press, 1977); and James M. Buchanan, Charles K. Rowley, and Robert D. Tollison, eds., *Toward a Political Economy of the Deficit* (Oxford: Basil Blackwell, forthcoming).

12. See, for example, Herman B. Leonard, *Checks Unbalanced: The Quiet Side of Public Spending* (New York: Basic Books, Inc., 1986).

"borrowing" does not show up in the standard measures of the deficit and public debt.

Let me give you a few examples. The federal role in credit markets is enormous. Credit assistance is extended to a long list of beneficiaries, including farmers, homeowners, exporters, small businesses, and rural utilities, to name a few of the more prominent ones. At the end of FY 1985, the federal government held $257 billion in its loan portfolio and had guaranteed loans totaling $410 billion. [13]

Clearly, the government's credit programs are a way of achieving social goals that otherwise could be achieved by direct spending. The subsidy-equivalent value of these loans and loan guarantees, estimated to be about $16 billion in FY 1985, is not included in the budget totals, however. [14]

Let me give you another example. The federal government operates several major insurance companies. The most important of these supply insurance to depository institutions, namely, banks and savings and loan companies. But others, such as the one that provides pension insurance, are also important. These programs involve immense potential liabilities and payments for future taxpayers. Moreover, they are often structured in a way that induces the insured firms to take risks that further increase taxpayers' exposure. Like credit assistance, none of these future liabilities shows up in our budget totals.

Let me recount one final example, though there are many others. Even as we have been dismantling the antiquated economic regulatory structure, which inhibited competition in a number of important industries for many years, we have erected an elaborate new social regulatory structure that diverts economic resources in the pursuit of a variety of public goals. Most of these goals are worthwhile, but the resources we spend on them, estimated to be between $50 billion and $150 billion annually, for the most part do not show up on our financial ledger. [15]

That government has grown in areas hidden from public view should come as no surprise. It is consistent with the incentive structure faced by our elected representatives, a matter to which I shall

---

13. See *Special Analyses, Budget of the U.S. Government, 1987* (Washington, D.C.: U.S. Government Printing Office, 1986), Special Analysis F; and *Economic Report of the President* (Washington, D.C.: U.S. Government Printing Office, 1986), chapter 6.

14. *Special Analyses*, pp. F-31–38.

15. See *Budget of the United States Government, FY 1987* (Washington, D.C.: U.S. Government Printing Office, 1986), p. 6a–17.

return in a moment. It is, moreover, a problem that might be expected to worsen during an era of budgetary stringency.

No Consensus on What Government Should Do

Part of the problem is that there are no widely accepted criteria, or even a common frame of reference, for determining what government should do and what it should not do. This is not to say that there are no common themes for government's role in this country. Almost everyone agrees that national defense, some forms of welfare, enforcement of contracts, and so forth should be provided—or at least financed—collectively. But within a fairly broad range, public opinion is divided, with "common sense" being perhaps the only underlying identifiable goal.

And lest we economists pat ourselves too firmly on the back for being above all this, with somehow having access to "truth" in matters of public policy, let me ask you, What is the economist's position on the details of national defense, such as the strategic defense initiative, antisatellite testing, chemical warfare, and the proposed missile build-down? Do Gordon Tullock and Kenneth Boulding agree? What about welfare reform? Does Jack Meyer's comprehensive plan mesh with the vision of John Kenneth Galbraith? Or on monetary policy, who is more nearly right: Beryl Sprinkel, Arthur Burns, or Craig Roberts? It may be the case that, unlike most other people, economists can fairly quickly determine the precise nature of their disagreements. But we still do disagree. And, as Paul Samuelson once put it: "If economists cannot agree among themselves, how can the world be expected to agree with them and to respect their recommendations?"[16] Or, as a Mal cartoon published in the *Washington Post* put it recently: "Which economist should we listen to today?"[17]

What is more, economists tend to hold policy views very strongly, though not as strongly as some who come to such views by means of religious conviction. The reason is that we economists pride ourselves on being objective analysts—knowledgeable about human behavior, marshalled with the facts, and sufficiently detached so that our own values will not interfere. I don't say it is true; I just said we think of ourselves in those terms.

I know from personal experience that this propensity on the part of economists to hold policy views firmly makes it difficult for us to

16. Joseph E. Stiglitz, ed., *The Collected Scientific Papers of Paul A. Samuelson*, vol. II. (Cambridge: The MIT Press, 1966), p. 1628.

17. *Washington Post*, October 5, 1986.

perform effectively in upper echelons of government, where trades and compromise are the name of the game, and the economist's job, unfortunately, is more that of fashioning a "good deal" than getting his or her way.

I was reminded of this recently when I was watching a TV program on George Washington.[18] The program dealt with the problems Washington faced as the first president and the way he handled them and the conflicts between the factions led by Hamilton and by Jefferson. Hamilton, believing himself to be a failure in government, eventually submitted his resignation to Washington, telling him, "I lack the politician's skill at compromise. Truth is truth and can't be halved."

Despite this difficulty, I do believe that economists' common training provides a methodology for trying to figure out the "right" answer. Frankly, I think it is a great advantage for a public official to have such a framework at his or her disposal, although, as I have mentioned, it does sometimes make it difficult to do jobs that require a lot of compromise. Moreover, such training is not sufficient to yield the "right" action when incentives are overpowering. Let me illustrate.

At one Friday afternoon seminar at the University of Virginia, our speaker was a new congressman who had been a classmate of Warren Nutter and Jim Buchanan at the University of Chicago and who, of course, had learned the lessons of microeconomics from Alfred Marshall and other good price theorists. After this congressman finished his spiel about "life in Washington," one of the bright young graduate students in the audience—who, by the way, is now a very successful Washington-based analyst—asked, "Why in the world would the Congress of the United States enact minimum wage legislation?"

This congressman, who had been in business for many years between graduate school and public service and who probably had not given a lot of thought to the formal analytics of the issue for many years said, "Oh, I understand." And going to the blackboard, he quickly pointed out equilibrium price and employment and showed the effects of a minimum wage, including the adverse effects on employment. He also demonstrated how a minimum wage could be a device to discourage business from moving from high-wage areas to low-wage areas. After thus showing us that his analytical tools were anything but rusty, he said, "I understand all of that very well. But I

18. *George Washington: The Forging of a Nation*, CBS Network Television, September 21–22, 1986.

11

represent a heavily unionized district in the north, and if you think I'm going to vote against minimum wage legislation, you're crazy."

Why Does Government Do What It Does?

In the absence of any generally accepted criteria (whether designed by economists or not) for judging what is an appropriate government function, virtually all areas of activity are fair game. Given the incentives faced by our elected officials, this is a difficult situation.

As is obvious, our federal government has the ability to transfer vast amounts of wealth through its policies. Given this ability, it is natural for groups in society with similar interests to band together and to expend economic resources to try to get some of that wealth moved in their direction.[19] Such groups can be successful because our agents in the political process, our elected representatives, do not feel the full costs and benefits of their actions. This is perhaps the fundamental reason why the political process has great trouble allocating economic resources efficiently.

As is by now a well-known story—thanks to Jim Buchanan, Gordon Tullock, Mancur Olson, and others—politicians have an incentive to transfer wealth to identifiable groups because the benefits are concentrated and the costs, paid by taxpayers in general, are diffuse.[20] Moreover, the beneficiaries are generally well informed about their programs and who supports them, while those who shoulder the burden are generally not so well informed, because it is not worth their while. Politicians have an incentive to search for such issues, where well-organized groups gain and the costs are borne by everyone. Groups with similar objectives have an obvious incentive under these circumstances to organize to obtain the benefits government can provide.

Because the ability of groups to influence the political marketplace depends on the costs of being organized, established groups have a particular advantage. They are able to act quickly when their programs are threatened, and this explains why it is so difficult to eliminate or even reduce existing programs. Unfortunately, our rec-

<hr />

19. For a review of this literature, see Robert D. Tollison, "Rent Seeking: A Review," *Kyklos* (1982), pp. 575–602.

20. See James M. Buchanan and Gordon M. Tullock, *The Calculus of Consent: Logical Foundations of Constitutional Democracy* (Ann Arbor: University of Michigan Press, 1962); and Mancur Olson, Jr., *The Logic of Collective Action: Public Goods and the Theory of Groups* (Cambridge: Harvard University Press, 1965).

ord this year bears this out. Last February, the president's budget proposed eliminating forty-four programs, and it appears we will be successful in terminating only two of them.

Let me recount one incident that demonstrates the ability of organized groups to protect their programs. One of our major budget themes has been privatization, and as part of this we proposed privatizing the five Federal Power Marketing Administrations (PMAs), which account for about 6 percent of the power generated in this country. Of course, the great majority of power is privately generated. Although, in general, private production is less costly than public production, the customers of the federal PMAs get their power at rates substantially below those available in the rest of the country. The reason is that the PMAs are subsidized by the general taxpayer.

Shortly after the PMA privatization proposal appeared in the FY 1987 Budget, the American Public Power Association and the National Rural Electric Cooperative Association (NRECA) mounted a national lobbying campaign, which eventually induced Congress to pass an appropriations rider banning any studies or proposals for transferring the PMAs[21] or the Tennessee Valley Authority out of federal ownership. This prohibition became law as part of the urgent supplemental for 1986.

By the way, the NRECA, which was a part of this lobbying campaign, is the same organization that makes it virtually impossible to cut back subsidized Rural Electrification Administration (REA) loans to "rural" utilities and telephone companies. You will recall that REA was passed back in the 1930s to bring electricity and telephone service to the rural parts of the country, a task that was completed some time ago. The subsidy, however, goes on and on.

Incentives and the Deficit

Given the incentives faced by elected officials, democratic governments will tend to engage not only in too much government spending, but also in excessive deficit financing of public expenditures.

Perhaps the basic difference between resource allocation decisions made in the marketplace and decisions made in a political setting is that market decisions are made with respect to well-defined, transferrable property rights, while political decisions are not.[22] None

---

21. The Alaska PMA was excepted.

22. See, for example, Dwight Lee, "Deficits, Political Myopia and the Asymmetric Dynamics of Taxing and Spending," in Buchanan, Rowley, and Tollison.

of us, as citizens, can sell shares in our government if we feel the wrong decisions are being made. This leads our elected officials to be myopic, that is, to operate with a discount rate that is too high.

In the market, the effect on future profitability of a manager's current decisions is reflected quickly in the price of the company's stock. Shareholders' ability to buy and sell stock provides an immediate test of the wisdom of corporate managers' decisions. In a political setting, there is no comparable indicator of the future effects of officials' decisions. Therefore, they will discount the future excessively, leading them to finance spending in excess of what citizens are willing to pay for out of current taxes.

This political myopia also explains why many of our expenditure programs are structured in a way that the costs of the programs start off modestly and then increase dramatically. Such an arrangement simultaneously benefits the political decision makers, with their excessively high discount rate, and the program beneficiaries, who presumably have a lower, more realistic rate. Rising expenditure patterns for government programs, of course, are also caused by the fact that interest groups find it easier to organize around an existing program. Once organized, they will tend to acquire more influence through time.

Thus, large deficits are the logical outcome of individuals pursuing their self-interest within the existing institutional framework. With the exception of future taxpayers—many of whom are not yet of voting age and many of whom have not yet been born—deficits create many winners and few losers. Politicians can generate support by increasing expenditures or cutting taxes, either of which directly benefits some group. Every legislator is in a position to try to confer such benefits on his or her favorite constituencies, and the incentive for any individual legislator to refrain from such behavior is virtually nonexistent. To do so would involve forgoing specific political support, without materially affecting the deficit.

Running deficits is easy because it makes people feel wealthier. Borrowing by an individual, in this sense, is quite different from borrowing by governments. An individual who borrows to buy a car, for example, does not feel wealthier relative to someone who pays cash, because he knows full well that he will have to reduce consumption in the future in order to pay off the loan. The liability for public debt, however, is dispersed throughout society and is not assigned to anyone in particular. This leads us all to underestimate the costs of deficit-financed spending. And as with any activity where the benefits are personal and the costs are social, deficit financing leads to too much spending. Taxpayers believe public services have become relatively cheaper, so they demand more of them. The true cost of public services has not changed, of course. If we were to pay for public services as we consume them, we would want less of them.

For the same reason that politicians have an incentive to run deficits, they also have an incentive to pursue goals through off-budget or regulatory programs. The costs of our regulatory programs, while substantial, are paid for in the prices of thousands of products purchased by consumers who have little idea that part of the price is going to pay a government-imposed cost. Many of our credit and other programs create future liabilities in the same way borrowing does. But in contrast to direct borrowing, these future liabilities are virtually invisible and are not even part of the political debate.

Gramm-Rudman-Hollings

All of the foregoing suggests that our political institutions, as historically structured, may not be capable of solving the problem of a government that is too big and is financed at the expense of future generations. Rather than give up in despair, we need to modify our institutions and place meaningful constraints on political behavior.

One such change occurred last year with the passage of the Balanced Budget and Emergency Deficit Control Act of 1985, better known as Gramm-Rudman-Hollings (GRH). GRH represents a major innovation on our political landscape and, in my view, has had a very important effect on the budget as well as on the budget process. To most of us who deal with such matters, it comes as no surprise that this scheme was designed by an economist—Phil Gramm.[23]

GRH was passed with great fanfare because elected officials, who find it very easy to vote for any new spending program, find it very difficult to vote against a law that requires balancing the budget. As we all know, GRH mandates that the budget be brought into balance over a five-year period. As originally passed, the most noted feature of the act was its "club in the closet"—its automatic provision that mandated across-the-board cuts in much of the budget if the normal political process did not achieve the specified, declining levels of the deficit. That provision caught all the headlines. The version of the automatic trigger Congress enacted was held to be unconstitutional by the Supreme Court, however, because it required the

---

23. A similar scheme was advanced by another economist, Martin Anderson. See Anderson, "The Budget Amendment—Not So Crazy after All," *New York Times*, August 30, 1985.

comptroller general, an official subservient to the Congress, to perform what was clearly an executive function.

Because the constitutionality of the comptroller general's role in executive functions had been challenged earlier, and because in negotiations on behalf of the administration I insisted, Congress included in the act a fallback procedure under which any automatic cuts that might be necessary to meet the mandated deficit limits would have to be put on a fast track for approval by the House and the Senate in a joint resolution to be presented to the president.

This fallback procedure obviously makes any necessary cuts less automatic, and when the Court made its ruling many people were less confident that any such cuts, in fact, would be made. Well, what has happened?

The first thing Congress did after the Court's decision was to reaffirm the FY 1986 sequester of $11.7 billion, using the fallback procedure. This, however, was not surprising inasmuch as most of the pain of those cuts had already been experienced by beneficiaries.

With respect to the FY 1987 Budget, the process I most wearily hope will be completed soon, Congress appears to have come up with a budget deficit below the GRH trigger level, at least the way the deficit must be measured according to GRH. Thus, there will be no sequester. Moreover, the Senate at least attempted to "fix" the automatic trigger by giving the director of the Office of Management and Budget (OMB)—yours truly—the final say so. So far, the House has not agreed.

This, however, should not cloud the success we are likely to experience this fiscal year with respect to both the deficit and total spending. The FY 1986 deficit was some $221 billion, an all-time record in real, as well as in nominal, terms. For FY 1987—the first full year that GRH is operative—I expect, when all is said and done, the deficit to come in under $170 billion. Although that figure exceeds the $144 billion GRH target by $26 billion, it means that in just one year we will have reduced the deficit by at least $51 billion *without raising taxes.*

As a percentage of GNP, the deficit will decline from 5.3 percent in FY 1986 to a projected 3.8 percent in FY 1987. The reason for this decline is that for the main part spending increases will be held at bay—a remarkable achievement, *especially* during an election year. Over the period FY 1980 through FY 1986, federal spending increased at an average annual rate of 3.6 percent in real terms; this year it will actually *fall* in real terms by approximately 2.4 percent. While a portion of this spending (and deficit) decline for FY 1987 can be traced to lamentable cutbacks in the president's request for defense and in-

ternational affairs, the message of the figures just cited holds up even
for domestic spending: rather than rising at the FY 1980 through FY
1986 average annual rate of 1.4 percent in real terms, this coming year
domestic spending will fall by about 3.0 percent in real terms.

In sum, GRH has changed the rules of the game, at least for this
year. We now have replaced President Carter's, ill-fated—sounds
good in theory; doesn't work in practice—"zero-based budgeting"
with what I call "zero-sum" budgeting. Anyone proposing a new
spending measure must come up with some way to finance it, either
a spending offset somewhere else or an increase in revenues. This
coming year not only will the deficit be lower, but also federal spending (in real terms) will actually decline.

One reason Congress complied with the requirements of GRH
during its first year is that the political pressures to do so were substantial. It would have been quite embarrassing, only months after
passing the law, not to meet its requirements. As time goes on, however, it is reasonable to expect those pressures to weaken. And, as
many have noted, what Congress does, it can undo. That is why, in
my view, we need to look toward more permanent, constitutional
solutions to the problem.

Constitutional Approaches

A permanent solution to the problem of excessive government
spending and borrowing requires a constitutional change to restore
the discipline we had for most of our history.

In the absence of the type of commitment implied by a constitutional change, individuals have less reason at any particular time
to undergo the sacrifice required to reduce spending or balance the
budget. Why should we, in 1986, reduce spending, knowing that
next year or the year after a new political coalition could make the
sacrifice we have undergone virtually meaningless? If, however, individuals could be assured that their current sacrifice would be reflected in permanent increases in future disposable income, they
would be much more willing to make such a sacrifice.[24]

Along with President Reagan and 71 percent of the American
public, I also support a line-item veto.[25] A line-item veto would enable
the chief executive to excise some of the most flagrant special-interest

---

24. See James M. Buchanan, "The Budgetary Bias in Post-Keynesian Politics: The Erosion and Potential Replacement of Fiscal Norms," in Buchanan,
Rowley and Tollison.

25. See "Line-Item Veto," *Gallup Report* (October 1985).

spending that all contemporary presidents have been forced to accept in the context of more general spending bills. One possibility might be to provide the president with sufficient line-item veto authority to bring the budget into balance or, in the short run, to meet the GRH deficit targets. This would be a better fix than giving sequester authority to OMB. Another possibility would be to guarantee the president an up-or-down vote on proposed rescissions.

Of course, I am aware that recent evidence from the state level indicates that line-item veto authority does not affect total borrowing (and by implication total spending), suggesting that such authority is used to reorder priorities.[26] But there are differences between the federal and state budgets, and besides, giving the president more authority to reorder priorities is not such a bad idea.

Now that we have settled these global issues, let's think on just a few mundane problems of application. For example, if we are going to require a balanced budget, which budget should be balanced? Our current budgeting methodology has been criticized on a variety of grounds, but one that is made most often is that it is an *operating* budget. Why not institute a capital budget? Proponents of a capital budget point out that investments in long-term assets should be amortized over time, as they are in the private sector and in most state and many local governments. Moreover, since capital assets have a long useful life, borrowing to finance them is justified.

I agree completely. It really does not make a lot of sense to treat capital expenditures the same as operating expenditures, which is what we do now. In many cases, doing so creates a misleading impression of the financial consequences of government decisions and distorts the decision-making process. Accordingly, we in the administration are now in the process of studying these issues and developing proposals to reform our financial accounts and the budget process. I fully expect the president to announce specific changes and legislative proposals in early 1987.

But I must tell you, establishing and maintaining the integrity of a capital budget are not as easy as they sound. First, as New York City experienced, there will be increasing, relentless pressure to transfer expenditures from the operating budget to the capital budget, in order to realize benefits now and postpone costs. Second, aside from incentives, there will be the knotty technical problem of classifying certain programs: which belong to the operating budget, and which belong to the capital budget? What about support for

---

26. See Charles K. Rowley, William F. Shughart II, and Robert D. Tollison, "Interest Groups and the Deficit," in Buchanan, Rowley, and Tollison.

higher education—is it an operating expense, or is it human capital? As a practical matter, how do we amortize nuclear submarines or historic buildings such as the Capitol and the White House?

But the strongest argument against a capital budget, in my opinion, is that given any opportunity to bypass conventional concerns over the deficit, such as posed by a capital budget, our elected officials may simply spend more money and government will grow even more. With the advent of the institutional changes posed by GRH, however, and the possibility of enactment of some form of enhanced rescission authority or line-item veto—and maybe action on a constitutional amendment to control deficits, taxing, or spending—I am more optimistic that establishment of a capital budget would not lead to this adverse consequence. And even if at the margin there were some tendency to increase spending, we must also consider the efficiency gains that a more "businesslike" approach to federal spending and financing decisions could generate.

Concluding Remark

Let me conclude now with an observation and a speculation.

Toward the end of his life, Warren Nutter became increasingly pessimistic about the future of Western institutions. Not only did he see the threat of monolithic Communism, but also he feared that America's leadership was in peril, threatened by a loss of confidence and resolve.

If Warren Nutter were alive today, I think he would be much more hopeful. The repair of our national defense has been nothing short of dramatic. And the restoration of America's self-confidence and its will to lead the free world into the twenty-first century is so self-evident that it is not even contested by what Jeane Kirkpatrick termed the "blame-America-first crowd." Such "revolutions" in thinking and in action are not likely to fade, at least not right away. So, I submit that if Warren Nutter were here among us, he would say, "I'm beginning to believe that everything's going to be all right."